LES TRÈS RICHES HEURES DU DUC DE BERRY

LES TRÈS RICHES HEURES DU DUC DE BERRY

15th – Century Manuscript

Texts by
Edmond Pognon

Chief Curator
Bibliothèque Nationale, Paris

Translated by David Macrae

Crescent Books
A division of Crown Publishers, Inc.

John of France, duke of Berry, being the son of King John the Good, brother of Charles V and uncle of Charles VI, was necessarily involved in the major events of those turbulent reigns. Yet the only thing that really interested him was the accumulation of splendid things of all sorts. Such an enterprise required vast funds: in order to acquire them he yielded absolutely to the temptations offered by the powers conferred on him by his birth. The county of Poitiers, which his father had given him as a fief when he was sixteen, in 1536; Berry, which was made into a duchy-peerage specially for him four years later—at a time when Poitou seemed entirely devoted to the English cause; Languedoc, of which he held the lieutenancy for several years of his brother's reign, and which was returned to him, despite the unpleasant memories he had left behind him, as soon as his nephew acceded to the throne—all of these territories were, for the duke, predominantly sources of revenue, which he exploited to the full. When in 1392 Charles VI had gone mad, the duke, together with his other nephew, Louis, duke of Orleans, found himself free to loot the whole of the kingdom for what it was worth. The lower classes hated him; when civil war broke out in France after the assassination of Louis by the fanatical followers of the duke of Burgundy, John the Fearless, he declared his support for the party of the Armagnacs; the Parisians, being "Burgundians", then launched an offensive against him. In 1411, gangs led by the butcher Legoix left the town by the St James Gate and set fire to his magnificent château of Bicêtre.

This must have been highly disconcerting to the duke. Worse was yet to come: before the end of that same year he lost, successively, his châteaux of Etampes and Dourdan, besieged and captured by his grand-nephew the dauphin Louis, whom John the Fearless had won over to his side and had under his close control.

One cannot really say, however, that the duke had no roof over his head. He still had, at Bourges, the "Royal" Palace which was his ducal residence; at Poitiers, which he had won back from the English in 1369, he had a palace, and, just out of town, the château of Clain; he had residences of legendary beauty such as his châteaux of Mehun-sur-Yèvre and Lusignan, as well as those of Nonette, Usson, Gien, Montargis and Boulogne-sur-Mer; a palace at Riom; near Graçay-en-Berry the Hôtel de Genouilly; at Bercy, the Hôtel de Giac, also known as the Grange-aux-Merciers; and in Paris itself a town house known as the Hôtel de Nesle. These, with the three dwellings he had just lost in 1411, make a grand total of seventeen.

It is very sad that nothing, or virtually nothing, now remains of these buildings. The pictures of some of them which are contained in this book gives one an idea of the magnitude of this loss—which is part of a pattern of similar destruction which was generally the fate of civil buildings in the Middle Ages. Their beauty and charm would provide attenuating circumstances in the favor of a man whose thirst for loot at the expense of the people was insatiable. After all, there are still rulers in the world today who keep entire nations in poverty—and do so much more effectively than him. They are doing so to satisfy their ideology. One is entitled to feel that the duke of Berry's motives were preferable. The fact that he was the first great patron of the arts of his period, and in fact the first of all the great European patrons, makes it possible to forgive many things.

The parchment embellished by this tireless collector of beautiful works has fared much better than his large collections of objects made of stone, gold and silver, jewelry, enamel and tapestry.

While patronizing all the arts, the duke of Berry was particularly well disposed to those whose talents as calligraphers or painters produced beautiful books. The inventory of his property mentions more than a hundred and fifty manuscripts, all of which were more or less richly illuminated. About a third of them were historical works, one fifth novels of chivalry; there were a few volumes on astrology, astronomy and geography. About half of the total number were religious books: Bibles, Psalters, breviaries, Missals, and, lastly, Books of Hours, of which there were fifteen.

A Book of Hours was a collection of prayers for use by the laity, or at least by those lay persons who wished, like the priests and monks, to address themselves to God at certain fixed hours of the day. The prayers vary with the time of the year; moreover, one or more saints are honored every day. For this reason, Books of Hours usually open with a calendar, each page of which occupies at least a page. Quite early on, it became customary to evoke, usually in a rather summary picture, the kind of human occupation most commonly associated with each month. This *hors d'œuvre* is followed by the *Hours*, consisting of prayers in honor of the Virgin, the Hours of the Cross, of the Holy Ghost and of the Passion, separated by pages containing extracts from the Gospels, the Psalms, the Litanies and the "proper', of certain masses. The volume also includes various prayers and pious exercises, scattered throughout the text.

Some Books of Hours were portable and could be read as one walked along. Those of the duke of Berry, however, were quite different. Most of them are far too big to be carried, and all of them were executed in such a luxurious manner that they were clearly intended for perusal by bibliophiles in the seclusion of their protected libraries. This fact of itself is sufficient to relegate the pious origins of the Books of Hours to a very secondary role. As one reads through them—and this one in particular—one feels even further removed from the spiritual tranquility which they are supposed to inspire. One

is moved deeply and intensely, it is true, but not with religious emotion as such. The sentiment aroused by this work is essentially one of aesthetic enjoyment.

If one takes a closer look at these *Très Riches Heures du duc de Berry*, which are now preserved in the Musée Condé, at Chantilly, one quickly becomes aware that the person glorified by this book is not the Lord: it is the duke. Starting with the very first month, January, the calendar shows us him seated at table, surrounded by an army of courtiers. Where tradition would have allotted a simple medallion to the scene of a man eating and making merry, here we are treated to a vast scene covering a whole page. In several of the other months, which are all given the same lavish treatment, the setting is provided by one of the duke's châteaux. In the body of the book, it is true, his august person is not unduly prominent; his coats of arms, his mysterious VE emblem, his bear and his stabbed swan —which are thought to be the basis for a pun on the name *Ursine,* a woman the duke once loved—appear only rarely. Yet the splendor of the pictures, the unbridled inventiveness of the architecture, the dress and the retinues makes it very hard for one to forget that these artists were working for a master who valued visual pleasures above all else— and particularly above meditation on the profound mysteries of Christianity. This is not the "luxury for God" with which the sacred art of the Middle Ages was so lavish. Here, despite the nature of the subject-matter, the reader can hardly escape the conclusion that God was the last thing the artists were thinking about.

Now a word about the artists, in the plural: several of them contributed to the making of the *Très Riches Heures,* and it is not always an easy task to attribute individual miniatures to any particular artist.

The posthumous inventory of the duke's property contains an entry which, it is unanimously agreed, concerns the *Très Riches Heures:* "Item: one box several notebooks of a *Très Riches Heures,* done by Pol and his brothers, very richly annotated and illuminated." This means that in 1416, the year of the duke's death, the book was in the process of being made, but still in the form of unbound sheets; the paintings which already existed were the work of several brothers, one of whom was called Pol. Before identifying these artists, we should note that the manuscript is now completed, and that the paintings which brought it to fulfilment differed markedly from the earlier ones. Seventy-five years ago, Paul Durrieu established that they were the work of a painter from Berry named Jean Colombe, from whom they had been commissioned by Duke Charles I of Savoy. In one of them the picture of this nobleman was placed facing that of Blanche of Montferrat, whom he had married in 1485. This means that the work of Jean Colombe may be dated somewhere

yrieleison.

xpeleison.

yrieleison.

piste audi nos.

ater de celis deus.

miserere nobis.

ili redemptor mūdi
deus miserere nobis

piritus sancte dns
miserere nobis.

ancta trinitas
unus deus miserere n.

ancta maria ora
pro nobis.

ancta dei genitrix
ora pro nobis.

ancta uirgo uir
ginum. ora pro nob.

ancte michael. ora

ancte gabriel. ora

ancte raphael. ora

geli z archangeli dei. ora

ancte iohannes
baptista ora

Omnes sancti patriar
che et prophete dei ora

ancte petre ora

ancte paule ora

ancte andrea. ora

ancte iacobe ora

ancte iohes ora

ancte philippe. ora

ancte thoma ora

ancte iacobe ora

ancte mathee. ora

ancte thadee ora

ancte bartholome
c. ora pro nobis. ora

ancte mathia. ora

ancte marce. ora

ancte luca. ora

ancte barnaba. ora

...ncte symon ora

between that year and 1489, the year when Charles I died. The *Très Riches Heures* were thus finished about seventy years after the death of John of Berry, and after they had been left in an incomplete state by the original artists.

The hand of Jean Colombe—about whom research which is still confidential is now being conducted—can be clearly recognized in the manuscript. His predecessors, on the other hand, pose more than one problem.

It is true that "Pol and his brothers" have long been identified. They were the sons of a sculptor on wood from Nimègue, named Arnold de Limbourg, and, through their mother, they were nephews of Jean Malouel who, having worked for Queen Isabeau of Bavaria, finally became court painter to the duke of Burgundy. They were called Pol, Jean (Jannequin, Janneken) and Herman. Their presence at the duke's court is attested by numerous documents, between 1410 and 1415. One would probably have to go back to 1408 in the case of Pol, assuming, that is, that it is correct to identify him as the "German painter" then busy at work in the château of Bicêtre, whom the distinguished patron of the arts—who was prepared to do anything for his artists—tried to have betrothed to an eight-year girl whose father was a rich burger of Bourges named Le Mercier. Apparently, being forcefully kept in the château of Etampes despite the impotent protests of the Parlement in Paris, the poor girl had to resign herself to her fate. Lastly, it has been established that the three brothers died in 1416, the same year as the duke, in the prime of life.

Yet this bibliographical information does not help us to decide which of the three brothers did what in the *Très Riches Heures*. The only way to do this is to look at the paintings themselves; only then does it become evident that a fourth man, with a clearly distinguishable manner, is also involved.

A scrutiny of the calendar, which is where one should start, is most revealing. Leaving aside the painting of November, which is the work of Jean Colombe, those of January, April, May and August are obviously by the same hand: the hand of an artist who is madly in love with the courtly life, with its colors, its gold, its elegance, its luxury and its grandiose fantasies. For the sake of convenience we may call him the "Courtly Painter". It could not possibly have been this artist that painted the snowy landscape in February, or the rustic scenes of June and July. Here we find another painter whose manner is characterized particularly by the position of the legs of persons in the standing position, by the blue of certain garments and by the shape of a black female hairdo. For our purposes, he is the "Rustic Painter". Let us now take a look at Mars, October and December: in all three, an attentive eye cannot fail to notice the hand of an artist whose inspiration

differs sharply from that of the two others, especially in his novel treatment of the visual illusion. He has discovered and rendered something which they had overlooked: the shadows cast by figures and objects on the ground. Like the Rustic Painter, he paints the lower classes: but he does so with a compassionate tenderness, aware of their fatigue and the harshness of their lives. On the faces of the plowman in March, the sower in October and the dog-handler and groom in December these sentiments can be read like an open book. He paints a horse, yet it bears little resemblance to the aristocratic steeds in May and August. His space is exclusively his, whereas the other two have painted mere settings.

These settings, like the backgrounds of the "Master of the Shadows" who has just made his appearance, usually represent a château, as we have seen. The three painted by the Courtly Painter for April, May and August are distant, faintly blurred by their remoteness and occupy only the central part of the horizon. For June and July, the Rustic Painter, on the other hand, has placed his architecture much closer to the foreground, deploying it from one edge of his landscape to the other and striving to include all its details. This is the treatment accorded to the château in the painting for September, which we have not previously mentioned; yet the grape harvest scene which accompanies it is not the work of the Rustic Painter. This painting, which was left unfinished at the time of the deaths of the Limbourg brothers, must therefore have been completed by a hand which is now generally thought to have been that of Jean Colombe. It is all the more likely that this work was first entrusted to the Rustic Painter because, apart from the style of the château, it has a harvest scene, as do his paintings of June and July. A doubt persists, however, if one takes a close look at the little woman in red walking towards the châteaux with a flat basket on her head: she is not the work of the Rustic Painter nor of Colombe. She irresistibly calls to mind the small figures, unfortunately all of them male, whom we see walking around at the foot of the rampart in October. That work, however, was painted by the Master of the Shadows... One wonders, accordingly, whether he might not also have started September.

The architectural backgrounds of the three paintings which are assumed to be the work of the Master of the Shadows are also puzzling. While all three of them take up the whole breadth of the horizon, that of March is somewhat distant, an ochre-color—perhaps on account of its real color; it has the greatest possible number of details, yet their definition is blurred by distance. The one in October, however, is close, rather white, fully legible—and treated in exactly the same manner as the château of September, whose gilded spires curiously resemble themselves and no others... As for December, here we find several towers of which only the upper parts stick up above the dried, rust-colored foliage of a winter forest: they are depicted in great detail, but on a smaller scale than in the October château. But if one compares the three compositions as a whole, one realizes that the March landscape and the little persons moving about in it have a sort of naive quality which cannot be compared with the haughty mastery shown by those of October. In other words, while the plowman in the foreground in March—as well as the field where he has just made his furrows—is clearly by the same hand as the sower in October and the grooms in December, the countryside which stretches away behind him, with its architecture, terrain and persons, more closely resembles the setting past which the huntsmen ride in August—a work of the Courtly Painter. March, like September, is thus a painting which was left incomplete by a Limbourg and finished not by Jean Colombe but by the artist whom we have named the Master of the Shadows.

Before proceeding further, let us make it quite clear that there are no other paintings by this Master of the Shadows in the rest of the manuscript, and that his manner, being manifestly an advance on that of the Limbourg brothers, suggests that it should be dated somewhat later. This conclusion is confirmed by the dress of the little figures of the inhabitants of the town—who could be presumed to be in closer touch with the fashions of the day—who are to be seen in the background in October. They could certainly not be from a period earlier than the middle of the 15th century. As for the identification of this painter, whose contribution to the *Très Riches Heures* is thus situated a good thirty years before that work of Jean Colombe, nothing conclusive has so far been agreed: the only hypothesis proposed is most unconvincing.

So far we have met only two of the Limbourg brothers. In order to acquaint ourselves with the work of the third we must leave the calendar. Soon thereafter we come across a *St John on Pathmos* whose graphic qualities make it very comparable to the work of the Courtly Painter, though with subtlely different effects. The same impression is created, at first sight, by the next work, the *Martyrdom of St Mark,* and by those which, throughout the manuscript—not counting, for obvious reasons, those of Jean Colombe—deal with specifically religious subjects. There we would be dealing with a Limbourg who is more particularly dedicated to what we would now call "sacred art"; we might nickname him the Pious. Yet there is a double page, on which the *Meeting of the Magi* faces the *Adoration of the Magi,* which causes a really attentive eye to stop and look again. While the *Meeting* appears to be the work of the Pious Artist, the Adoration abruptly plunges us into the atmosphere of January, April and May; the

longer one looks at it, the more evident the hand of the Courtly Painter becomes. From then on, one's eye becomes keener. What about the *Purification,* should not that also be attributed to him? And the *Coronation of the Virgin?* And the *Fall of the Rebellious Angels?* In this way, right up to the end of the book, to *St Michael,* the last Limbourg painting, one's eye will try to divide authorship —more often than not without any certainty—between the Courtly and the Pious Painters.

These are some factors which might serve as a general chronology of the elaboration of the *Très Riches Heures.* Here, now, is one more such factor.

The nine châteaux or architectural complexes painted in the calendar may be divided, in the light of currently recognized identifications, as follows:

March: château of Lusignan. — April: château of Dourdan. — May: the Ile de la Cité, Paris (1). — June: the Ile de la Cité (2). — July: château of Etampes. — September: château of Saumur. — October: château of the Louvre. — December: château of Vincennes.

On the basis of the attributions proposed above, these monuments may be divided between the artists as follows:

Courtly Limbourg: Lusignan, Dourdan, Cité (1), Etampes.

Rustic Limbourg: Cité (2), Poitiers, Saumur (?).

Master of the Shadows: Louvre, Vincennes, Saumur (?).

It will be recalled that the châteaux of Etampes and Dourdan were taken by John the Fearless and the dauphin Louis at the end of 1411. It is true that the duke endured these reverses with a philosophical spirit—and even, judging by the gay life which he continued to live and to share with his beloved artists, the even more cruel loss of Bicêtre. Even so, it is not likely that the Courtly Painter painted these two châteaux after their fall. Firstly, the siege, at least in the case of Etampes, had caused severe damage. It should also be noted that Bicêtre, which was much more beautiful and a source of far greater pride for the duke, does not appear in the calendar, apparently because the painting still had not been made when it was burnt down in 1411. On the other hand, as Etampes and Dourdan *do* appear in it, they must have been painted before 1411. The château of Lusignan, which remained intact for many years more, must have been painted much later, since the painting was still not completed in 1416. For the Courtly Painter, therefore, there remains his view of the Cité, the various buildings of which show their rooftops and part of their gables and walls above the foliage of a spring forest. The duke had no residence there; but, it will be remarked, he did have a view of the island from his town house of Nesle. At any rate, there is no reason for assigning to this painting a date limit other than 1416.

Eus miſerat̄
nr̄i et benedicat
nobis illuminet uul
tum ſuum ſuper nos
et miſeratur n̄r̄.

Ut cognoſcamus in
terra uiam tuam in
omnibus gentibus
ſalutare tuum.

Confiteantur tibi

Nor can one stately precisely the dates of the Cité painted by the Rustic Painter and his château of Clain which, since it belonged to the duke, hardly needs a justification for its presence. The same is not true, however, of Saumur: without a doubt, Duke Louis II of Anjou, who had just finished building it, was the nephew of the duke of Berry, but he was not the only one. Their relationship thus explains nothing. It is surprising, however, that the Rustic Painter should have painted Saumur during his master's lifetime. But, as we have seen, we have good reason to think that this superb piece of architectural draftsmanship might have been the work of the Master of the Shadows. If that were so, there would be no further need to seek a justification for it on the duke's side. One more reason, therefore, in favor of the same attribution. At any rate, the two châteaux which were certainly painted by this artist, about whom we know nothing, are the Louvre and Vincennes, in other words, royal residences. It is tempting to speculate that, for this reason, the *Très Riches Heures,* after the death of the duke of Berry and before they reached the hands of the duke of Savoy, may have spent some time amongst the collections of the king of France. But the archival research involved in the exploration of such a hypothesis remains to be done.

In order to make this analysis of the *Très Riches Heures* slightly less incomplete—and we admit that, for the sake of brevity, we have neglected the small miniatures embodied in the text and ignored the highly variable form of the frames around the larger ones—we should point out that eight of the large miniatures of the manuscript were painted on independent sheets of parchment, which were then slipped into place among earlier sheets which had already been arranged in order. They are the following: Man and the Zodiac, Paradise on Earth, the Meeting and the Adoration of the Magi, the Purification, the Fall of the Rebellious Angels, Hell, and the Map of Rome. All of them are the work of the Limbourg brothers.

This manuscript, one of the most beautiful and the most famous of those left to us by the Middle Ages, cannot be traced exactly from one owner to the next since the death of the duke of Berry. As we have just seen, it must have found its way into the library of the king of France, though this is not confirmed by any document. We know that it belonged to Duke Charles of Savoy who entrusted the belated completion of the work to Jean Colombe. It was then inherited by Margaret of Austria, daughter of Emperor Maximilian. Then it vanishes from the records until the 18th century, when it was given a fine red Moroccan leather binding with the arms of Spinola. Baron Felix of Margherita, from Turin, inherited it. The duke of Aumale bought it from him in 1855. The *Très Riches Heures* was then placed by this great collector on the shelves of his library in the château of Chantilly, together with which it has, through a legacy, become the property of the Institute of France.

Edmond Pognon

P.S. — These observations, thoughts and hypotheses, personal, independent and non-conformist as they are, could not have been expressed without the earlier work done by the extremely learned Jean Longnon, who, for many years, watched over the *Très Riches Heures* in his capacity as Curator at Chantilly and profoundly studied it; or without the work of his successor Raymond Cazelles, who collaborated with him in the presentation of a superb complete reproduction of the manuscript, and who, in 1976, summarized all previous research in his excellent article in the *Revue française d'histoire,* entitled: "Les étapes de l'élaboration des *Très Riches Heures du duc de Berry*"; nor would my contribution have been possible without the work of Dr Eberhard König who, in a recent issue of the magazine *Archeologia,* was the first to draw attention to the innovating genius of the "Painter of October"—our Master of the Shadows—though, to be quite honest, he does not succeed in positively identifying him. **E.P.**

JANUARY

In the calendars of the Books of Hours January is portrayed as a jolly figure, his back to the fire and his belly to the table. The one shown here is none other than the duke of Berry, his profile, somewhat thickened by age, visible beneath a fur hat crowned by a single brilliant diamond. He does have his back to the fire—protected from the flames, however, by a wicker screen—and his belly to the table, and it is a well-stocked table, at which provision has also been made for his little dogs. His glory is complete: above his head is a canopy bearing his coat of arms, adorned with his bears and swans; behind it is a tapestry of a battle scene, possibly the one woven for him in 1385 in the great hall of the Royal Palace at Bourges (where the scene would thus be situated); in front of him is his magnificent 'Pavilion salt-cellar', whose golden brilliance is echoed, on the left, by several fine pieces of silverware; his pages, clad in sumptuous liveries, wait upon the duke; the chamberlain, meanwhile, beckons to the multitude of visitors who have doubtless come to offer their best wishes for the New Year, and also their gifts, and who perhaps hope, in turn, to receive some splendid gift from the duke. (Fol. 1v.)

FEBRUARY

February is shown as a merry individual warming himself in front of the fire, sometimes accompanied by a dog and a servant carrying firewood; here, however, the scene is enlarged to include a snow-covered landscape. By removing one of the walls of the house the artist has given us a picture of the interior and its occupants. The well-dressed lady in the foreground, raising her skirt just enough for the flames to warm her legs, averts her gaze in order not to see what her farmer and his wife, simple souls, are exposing to the fire. Outside, the sky is black and the earth white; the characters, animals, accessories and the building, both far and near, all reflect a winter which the artist himself must have experienced and contemplated profoundly. (Fol. 2v.)

MARCH

The traditional occupation of March in the calendar is the pruning of the vine. Here, in an enclosure, we see three vine-growers busy pruning, and, in another, a vine which has already been pruned. The unknown painter, whose style can also be recognized in October and December, has placed in the foreground a man steering his plow. The field which he is tilling is clearly the work of this artist, whereas the rest of the setting is apparently by one of the Limbourg brothers. On the far left, a shepherd is carrying a big bundle of grass in the midst of his sheep which are grazing in a meadow; a peasant is sifting grain into a sack. At the intersection of the road which separates these four scenes stands a Gothic edifice known as a montjoy. In the background one can see the first of the castles which are depicted in this calendar, the château of Lusignan; on top of its tower stands a gilded winged serpent, one of the forms taken by the foundress and protectress of the castle, the fairy Mélusine, whose legend had been recorded by Jean d'Arras, secretary to the duke of Berry, in a manuscript which is now in the library of Mehun-sur-Yèvre. The château of Lusignan was burnt to the ground in 1575. (Fol. 3v.)

APRIL

In all the calendars April is the month for picking flowers: the two elegant girls bending over the grass are doing precisely that. Yet they catch our eye less than the princely group to the left which has obviously been celebrating a betrothal. Various names have been suggested for these two lords and their ladies, though nothing has been said of the boy visible on the far left. The castle which can be seen on the horizon is probably the château of Dourdan, the foundations of which partly survive today. The body of water beneath it would thus be the river named the Orge, though the artist has painted what looks more like a pond. Note the interesting isometric projection of the orchard with its walled enclosure and the crenellated building on the right. (Fol. 4v.)

MAY

For May the artist has chosen boys and girls on horseback. He thus remains faithful to tradition, but has enlarged considerably on this theme, depicting a whole cavalcade, preceded by musicians blowing into a *buisine,* three flutes and a trombone; they wear a distinctive golden disk on their left shoulder. The horseman wearing blue and riding a grey horse with a red saddle cover could well be the duke as a young man; at least his little dogs, which are regularly shown with him, suggest that this might be so. The dresses of the three ladies in green who are riding behind him are of the bright shade of green customarily worn to celebrate the First of May. On such a beautiful day everyone is wearing green, as indeed they should: it is the green of the foliage which adorns their heads and necks — in fact the wild rose from which it was taken is not far away. The rooftops emerging from the leaves are those of the Palais de la Cité, in Paris. Even today it is possible to recognize here the clocktower and the towers of the Conciergerie. (Fol. 5v.)

JUNE

Haymaking is symbolic of June. On this left bank of the Seine, facing the Palais de la Cité which we see here a second time, but more completely rendered than under the month of May, it must be a very hot day, judging by the bare legs of the three reapers, the light dresses of the two girls winnowing the hay, and the hats and kerchiefs protecting their heads. The tall building with a cross on top is the Sainte-Chapelle. The large round tower with the pointed roof was the Montgommery Tower. The artist has enlivened his architectural settings by the use of tiny human figures: one is going up the three curved steps leading to the postern which overlooks the Seine, while a small crowd of people are climbing the covered staircase leading to the upper floor of the corner pavilion. (Fol. 6v.)

JULY

For the month of July the miniaturist has grouped together its usual theme, the harvest, and the shearing of the sheep, which, in those calendars which contain it, usually occurs in June instead of the haymaking. Note that, while fodder crops are being cut with a scythe, the cereals are cut with a sickle: this is because the stalks were to be cut only half-length, so that straw would be left in the fields for the cattle. The spring shears in the hands of the shearers are also worth noting. On the banks of the Clain, within sight of the château of Poitiers, it does not seem to be quite as hot as in June by the Seine: the workers, with one exception, are less lightly clad. The château of Poitiers, which was built for the young duke not far from the town, from which it was separated by a tributary of the Boivre, has now completely disappeared. (Fol. 7v.)

AUGUST

It seems that the calendar of the *Très Riches Heures* is the only one in which August is represented by a hunting scene—the usual theme being the threshing of the corn. Here two young nobles, their ladies riding pillion, are accompanied by a solitary lady on her white horse as they set out on a fowling expedition. The falcons, waiting on gloved fists, already seem quite excited. The unaccompanied lady is wearing a cloak identical to that worn, in May, by the young lord who could, in our opinion, be taken for the duke of Berry. The coincidence is surely not fortuitous, though the precise reason for it remains obscure. At the foot ot the château of Etampes, whose lofty Guinette tower, still visible today thougrh in ruins, is clearly recognizable the harvest is nearing completion: the sheaves are being piled up on a cart. The cool waters of the Juine, which flows nearby, has attracted four bathers; at least one of them is a woman who, already naked, has ventured only ankle-deep into the water. (Fol. 8v.)

SEPTEMBER

September calls for scenes of the grape harvest. Despite their independent frame of mind, the illuminators of the *Très Riches Heures* could not escape the trend. The vineyard chosen here is at Saumur, doubtless a better vintage than those which the duke had to hand at Berry or Poitou. The château, which we can recognize from what remains of it today, belonged to his nephew Louis II of Anjou, who had just had it built. Note the curious opaque fence around the vineyard: it seems to be made of woven and blackened wicker or reeds, though its purpose is uncertain. To the right stands a small montjoy, simpler than that shown in March, and in a later style. On the road leading to the château a woman dressed in red carries a basket on her head; to the left of the postern of the drawbridge is the tall chimney of the kitchen, similar to that of the nearby abbey of Fontevrault. (Fol. 9v.)

OCTOBER

Sowing is the classic theme for October. The painter whose mastery we had occasion to admire in March has here done even better, if such a thing were possible. He placed himself on the left bank of the Seine, opposite what is now the Palais de l'Institut, in other words opposite the Louvre which stands on the other bank in the state in which Charles V left it. Apart from the extraordinary accuracy of this architectural drawing, we should note the small figures walking along the quay, dressed in a style which is definitely later than the duke's declining years, the scarecrow in the form of an archer, his job made easier by feathers strung on a network of taut wires; note also the stone weighing down the harrow, the thieving magpies... The horse, although remarkably well drawn, is not walking the way horses do in real life: like all the artists of the Middle Ages, the painter of the month of October had not realized that horses, when walking, move the right front leg and the left hind leg forward at the same time. This observation also applies to the horses of the Limbourg which we have already seen in the months of May and August, and to those we shall shortly see in the *Meeting of the Magi*. (Fol. 10v.)

NOVEMBER

Here we have another perfectly traditional theme: the November acorn harvest, which Jean Colombe, seventy years after the work of the Limbourg brothers, has depicted without any additions. The acorns are ripe in that month, and the pigs, who spent more of their time in the open air than their modern counterparts, were very fond of them. In order to knock them down from the oak trees the swineherd is seen here throwing a stick up at the branches. His posture is remarkably well captured, but his face is ugly. The convention of medieval iconography required that peasants should be ugly. Jean Colombe observes this rule more obediently than the preceding illuminators of the *Très Riches Heures,* whose peasants, male and female, are painted with much tenderness. The coppice and the blueness of the remote horizon seen through the undergrowth are beautifully rendered. (Fol. 11v.)

DECEMBER

In December, in all the calendars, the slaughtering of pigs is shown. The master of the months of March and October has kept to the tradition, in his personal way: the victim is, in fact, a pig, but a wild version, or boar. And instead of being bled in a farmyard, it succumbs at the end of a long pursuit. This is the last act of a hunt with coursing dogs, the quintessentially noble sport, on which one is surprised not to find lordly gentlemen in the saddle. Instead, the artist has preferred to keep them to one side, choosing to focus on his favorite humble types: two grooms, one of whom is blowing the trumpet, and a bearded dog handler who is barely able to control his animals as they rush in for the kill. Above the forest, which is still rust-colored, one can see the towers of the château of Vincennes, enlarged by Charles V and very different from what it had previously been when, in 1340, Jean de France, the future duke of Berry was born there. (Fol. 12v.)

used to be exceedingly fond of this branch of learning. This picture seeks to illustrate the relationships between the human being and the signs of the Zodiac. In the four corners these signs are divided evenly among the four humors: choleric, melancholy, sanguine and phlegmatic. In the central oval are two strangely hermaphroditic figures. The one facing the viewer is usually thought of as being feminine; yet the narrowness of the hips, the breadth of the shoulders, the biceps and the firmness of the pectoral muscles make this unlikely, especially when one remembers that the artist does know how to depict the female body, as can be seen from his version of the Twins in the left margin. The figure with its back to the viewer has broader hips, more sloping shoulders and less muscular arms—clearly the more feminine of the two. The ambiguity persists and is surely intentional, though its motive escapes us. The only thing which is made quite clear is the attribution of a sign of the Zodiac to each part of the body.

This composition is found in no other Book of Hours. Even here it did appear in the original plan: it is the first of the eight separate plates. When one considers the relationship between the Zodiac and the solar year, it could be regarded as a supplement to the calendar. (Fol. 14v.)

MAN AND THE ZODIAC

The name usually given to this painting is "anatomical man". But here we are dealing with astrology, not astronomy. The duke of Berry, whose arms are to be seen at top right and left, with the mysterious sign VE below,

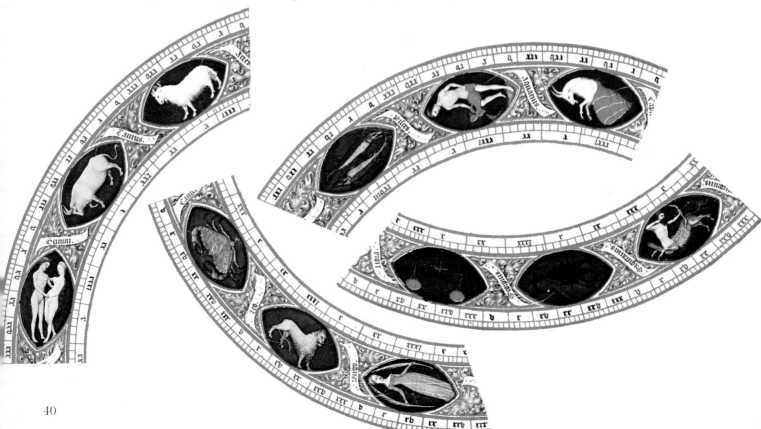

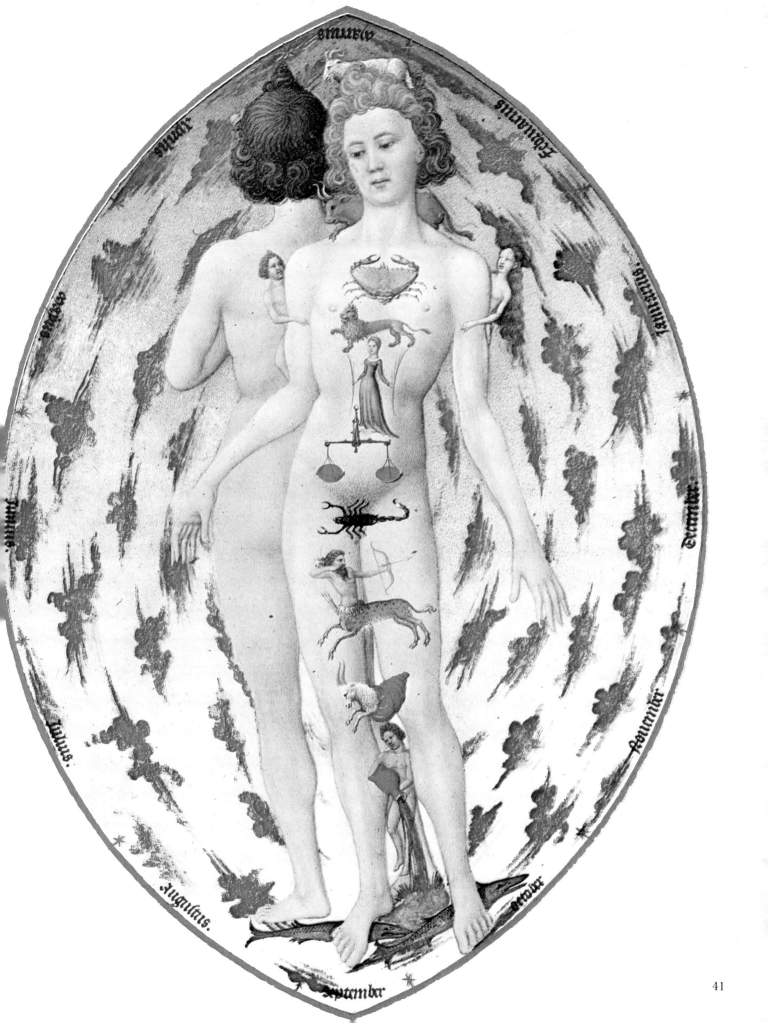

Aries

ffebruarius

martius

aprilis

December

Junius

Nouember

Maius

October

Julius

September

Augustus

41

SAINT JOHN ON PATHMOS

We now enter the text of the Book of Hours. It begins with extracts from the Gospels, hence the paintings of the evangelists.

Here we have Saint John who, as is well known, before writing his Gospel was exiled to the island of Pathmos where he had a vision which he later described in his Apocalypse. He heard trumpets and could already see the triumph of Christ, surrounded by the twenty-four elders crowned and dressed in white whom the artist has shown seated in choir-stalls, as if they were in church. The four red heads wrapped in yellow wings are four cherubim; a close look will reveal that each of them has three pairs of wings. The three trumpets are a slight excess, if they illustrate the 'voice loud as a trumpet' which was first heard by John, or perhaps too few in number if they are meant to represent the seven trumpets mentioned in Chapters VIII and IX. The red object in the eagle's beak is a traveling writing desk. (Fol. 17v.)

MARTYRDOM OF ST MARK

Another evangelist singled out for full page treatment is St Mark, here shown at the beginning of his martyrdom. The saint, who was preaching the Good Worrd in Alexandria, Egypt, was attacked by pagans at the foot of the altar where, as we can see from his chasuble, he was celebrating mass. The artist, who followed the account of this event given in the Golden Legend, has dressed his Egyptians in oriental style, but the streets of Alexandria, as seen by him, are lacking in local color. His urban architecture, the first we have seen in the manuscript, are distinctly Italian and reminiscent of the style of the masters of Florence and Sienna who greatly inspired the Limbourg brothers. (Fol. 19v.)

m   temerata et
me   ternum bene
dicta   singularis at

q̃ incomparabi   lis virgo dei geni

trix maria gratissimum dei templum spiritus sã
sacrarium ianua regni celorum. per quam post
deum totus uiuit orbis terrarum de te dei genitrix
filius dei uerus et omnipotens deus suam sacratis
simam fecat matrem assumens de illa sacratissiã;
carnē per quem mundus qui perditus erat salua
tus est. Cuius preciosissimo sanguine suo mundꝰ

redemptus est. et
omnia peccata
et remissa sunt
formans eam ĩ
preciosissimo sã
guine tuo inuenꝰ
eam eterne et in
commutabili
diuinitatis sue
a quo bona cūc
ta procedunt p

THE VIRGIN, THE SIBYL AND AUGUSTUS

The text and pictures on this page form an integrated whole. At the threshold of the Hours of the Virgin it is a hymn of praise to the glory of Mary, mother of the Savior. This is the meaning of the prayer— the only one in the whole book which is written on full lines rather than two columns. It is also the meaning of the three miniatures: the Sibyl, a pagan prophetess, is shown as a woman carrying a child, radiant as the sun, and whom a voice announces as the 'altar of the Son of God'; she tells Emperor Augustus, who has come to consult her, that a king more powerful than himself is about to be born. He believes her and adores the new king on trust. Like many Western artists, the painter has given the emperor the face of the emperor then reigning in Constantinople. (Fol. 22v.)

PARADISE ON EARTH

This miniature, the second of the eight full plates, is somewhat unusual in a Book of Hours; it should really be called "Original Sin'. Yet it is well situated, at the head of the prayers to the Mother of the Redeemer who has come to atone for Adam's sin. The composition of this picture is also exceptional: it has no rectangular border and runs directly into the white of the parchment, which is in stark contrast with the forbidding fence surrounding an exactly circular Paradise, symbolic of perfection. Outside this circle it is clearly possible only to wander helplessly in the midst of a hostile world. And that is precisely what was to happen to the first human couple when Eve, tempted by a handsome devil, shared with Adam the forbidden fruit. Both of them were condemned by God and expelled by the angel; in their nudity they felt no longer beautiful but shameful. The artist has given Eve the protruding belly which was considered fashionable for beautiful women of his day. Adam's anatomy, which is less influenced by the fashions of the time, is based on a Hellenistic statue which can still be seen at the Museum of Aix-en-Provence. (Fol. 25v.)

49

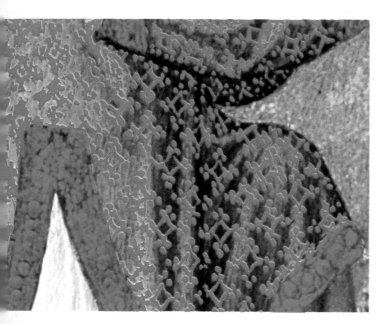

THE ANNUNCIATION

The announcement made by the Angel Gabriel to the Virgin Mary of her supernatural motherhood is a subject so closely linked to the mystery of the Incarnation that the manner in which it was to be depicted was carefully prescribed. At the very least the artist was required, for example, to place on the angel's arm a lily, symbolizing purity, and, in his other hand, a scroll on which his greeting, "*Ave gratia plena'*, is partly visible; the Holy Ghost, sent by God the Father in the form of a dove descending towards the Virgin while she unsuspectingly reads the Bible, is also a requisite feature. The artist's fantasy has taken refuge in the complicated architecture of the oratory, the angelic musicians assembled above the vault, and also in the decorative work in the margins, which is no longer confined to foliated scrolls springing out of the ornate initials but has taken the much freer form of small independent groups of angelic musicians, together with two coats-of-arms of the house of Berry, each held aloft by the bear and the swan so dear to the duke's heart. (Fol. 26v.)

omnie aratura alande

Onine diis
nr quam ad
mirabile est nomen tu
um in univerla tira.
Quoniam elevata
est magnifientia tua
super celos.
roie infantium

DAVID SEES CHRIST IN THE SPIRIT

Here is a sample of those pages of text in which the miniature takes up only a part of the two columns. In the small compositions the artist often uses decorative backgrounds—such as we have already seen behind the Sibyl and Augustus—rather than landscapes which would thus have been rather cramped. This one illustrates the 8th Psalm, the text of which reads as follows: 'Oh Lord, our Lord, how majestic is thy name in all the earth! Thy glory is above the heavens!" Nothing in the rest of the text accounts for the presence of the black African family facing King David, the author of this poem. The artist may, however, have wished to symbolize the human beings of the 'other end of the earth'. (Fol. 27v.)

THE VISITATION

The angel of the Annunciation had added: "Elizabeth, your relative, has conceived a son, in her old age and now she who had been thought barren is in her sixth month". Mary promptly went to the town of Judea, in the mountains, where her relative, the future mother of St John the Baptist, lived. As she greeted her, Elizabeth felt the child move within her, and, filled with the Holy Ghost, she cried out: "Blessed art thou among all women and blessed is the fruit of thy womb!" The artist presumed that, when she said these words, she bent her knee. Note also the town nestling among the mountains of the background landscape. He has taken the liberty of placing Elizabeth's house quite a long distance away, and has taken an even freer approach in the quite comical decorative detail in the margins. (Fol. 38v.)

cus madiu   dium me festina.
torium meū   Soria patri et filio
intende.   et spiritui sancto.
Domine ad adiuuā Sicut erat in prina

porcas cuis: in confcf
fione aua cuis inhym
nis confirmuni illi.
Laudate nomen ei
quoniam fuauis est
dominus meternum
mifencordia et ufq; in
generaaone et genera
aonem ueritas cuis.
Glona pri et filio ett.

Jubilate dco om
nis terra: fcui
te domino in le
naa.
Jntroite in confpe
ai cuis: in cultaaone.
Saate quoniam
dominus ipfe est deus
ipfe fecit nos et non ipi
nos.
Populus cuis et ou
es palcue cuis introit

DAVID IN PRAYER AND MEDITATION AT NIGHT

   This fine sample of a page containing two miniatures in the text is based on two of the Psalms.
The crowned Psalmist is clad in the sumptuous
pink robe which the artist puts him in whenever he
appears; he is first shown kneeling before an altar
bearing the Ten Commandments.   The curious
cone situated above them could not possibly be a
lantern, as some authors have claimed: its design is
such that the slightest flame would set it alight;
apart from which, it sheds no light.   It is probably
intended to focus reverent awe on the Commandments themselves, as a canopy might highlight the
dignity of some important person.   The miniature
illustrates the 100th Psalm: "Make a joyful noise
to the Lord, all the lands! Serve the Lord with
gladness!..."   The other depicts David having a
dream in which he sees the Resurrection of Christ;
it accompanies the 63rd Psalm, but does not follow
it very closely; the verse which is best suited to it
is the 6th: "When I meditate on thee in the watches
of the night". (Fol. 39v.)

tits ii iiiiiiiaii taii
omnis fines tiir. ⬛
Sloria patii et filio.

THE THREE HEBREWS IN THE FURNAGE

In the 7th century BC, when the Hebrews were under the domination of the king of Babylon, Nebuchadnezzar II, three of them refused to worship his statue. The king had them thrown into a furnace, but they felt no pain and could be heard singing a song of praise to the glory of the Eternal Lord. The version given in the Book of Daniel adds that a fourth person joined them in the furnace and that his face was that of one of the sons of the gods. Note the smoke which the artist has playfully added in the margin. (Fol. 40v).

enedicite omnia
opera domini
domino: laudate et su
pererultate eum in se
cula.

THE NATIVITY

This charming miniature combines all the traditional elements which are found, or at least *used* to be found until recently, among the components of the manger at Christmas. It also contains a few new ones: the four small blue angels in the form of birds clustered around the infant Jesus are rarely, if ever, found elsewhere. St Joseph, his age greatly exaggerated by his long grey beard, is wearing a pointed turban, like the Oriental that he is. The Father in his celestial glory and the Holy Ghost between heaven and earth, shed their radiance on the Son: the Trinity is complete and its mystery is blended with that of the Incarnation, which takes place at that very moment. (Fol. 44v).

THE ANNUNCIATION TO THE SHEPHERDS

Everything contained in this painting was already in the scene of the Nativity, but in the background. Here the shepherds and the angels regaling them with music at the cribside are the principal, if not the sole, subject. Note that, while the figures are painted with some realism, the landscape is highly stylized and only remotely resembles the evocative landscapes of the calendar. (Fol. 48).

THE MEETING OF THE THREE MAGI

Perhaps in order to compensate the duke for the shabby garb of the shepherds and the poverty of the manger, the illuminator here lavishes the wealth of his art and an unbridled orientalism on the sumptuous theme of the Three Magi. He deals with it twice rather than once: before showing them prostrating themselves before the child god, he also imagines them as their three retinues meet, guided by the star, after jong journeys from their respective kingdoms. As one might expect, the place where their paths cross is marked by a montjoy decorated with fine sculptures, further embellished with bronze statues. Artists always went out of their way to distinguish between Melchior, Balthazar and Gaspard; for example, Gaspard is often shown as a black. Here the distinction is essentially one of age. The oldest of the trio is Melchior, the black-bearded king is Balthazar and the smooth-chinned one Gaspard. On the horizon the illuminator has simply painted the City of Paris and the Butte Montmartre; further to the right, the château perched on top of a hill has a tower which is reminiscent of the tower of Montlhéry. Apart from this Parisian horizon, there is a painting by Gentile de Fabriano in the museum of the Accademia in Florence which is very similar; it is, however, dated 1423, or at least seven years later. Could the two artists have used the same model? (Fol. 51v.)

THE ADORATION OF THE MAGI

This Adoration of the Magi is much more customary than the Meeting which faces it. There is, however, a slight difference of style: the shapes in the Adoration are even more elegant, the colors more delicate and harmonies more subtle. Nonetheless, the painter has made the figures similar to those in the Meeting, and has dressed them in more or less the same clothes. There is nothing surprising in the presence of the shepherds in the background. The young women, two of them wearing halos, who are seen kneeling behind Mary are not so easily accounted for. They are doubtless saintly girls who have spontaneously come to help the mother of the baby Jesus and to add some comfort to the manger which is still her home and where we see her sitting on a carpet. The town in the distance is clearly Bourges. (Fol. 52).

THE PURIFICATION

Mary went to the Temple of Jerusalem to be "purified" and to present her child. St Luke quotes the text of the Law of Moses: "Each firstborn child shall be consecrated in the name of the Lord". A pair of turtles or two young doves were to be brought to the sacrifice. The artist has greatly enhanced the entrance to the sanctuary and managed to produce a majestic effect in this treatment of this simple theme. He has not made Mary herself carry the turtles: the magnificent woman who carries them in a basket as she ascends the stairs, with a candle in her other hand, seems to be detached from the group of women assembled behind the Virgin Mother, who watches her progress with evident interest. These are the same figures we have already seen in the crib scene during the Adoration of the Magi. It is almost as though the illuminator, unable to bear the stark isolation of the Mother of God, and unimpressed by her greatness, has hastened to surround her with maids of honor. The general layout of this miniatures recurs in several Italian works, most notably in a fresco in Santa Croce, Florence, depicting the Presentation of the Virgin; the original drawing for this painting, which is by Taddeo Gaddi, is now in the Louvre. (Fol. 54v).

THE HALT ON THE FLIGHT INTO EGYPT

We suddenly find ourselves disconcerted by the change to the syle of Jean Colombe, who lived seventy years later. This is an episode from the flight of the Holy Family into Egypt. During a halt, Mary noticed some tempting fruit on a tree. In response to the words of the child Jesus, the tree bent over so that Joseph could pick the fruit. The other figures, male and female, are inhabitants of the area. In the lower portion the artist has painted another legendary miracle performed by the child-God: while passing by a peasant who was sowing seed in his field, Jesus has himself thrown a handful of seed, whereupon the entire field became covered with ripe wheat. Herod's men then came that way and asked after the fugitives. "Yes, replied the peasant, I have seen them, just as I was sowing this wheat". (Fol. 57).

THE CORONATION OF THE VIRGIN

Note, in the midst of the angelic musicians, the one holding the crown and just about to place it on the Virgin's blond hair. The congregation includes, on the right, St Peter (pink robe, hands crossed on chest), with St Paul on his left; lower down, St Clair dressed as a nun; bottom left, after an unidentified bishop, St Francis and St Stephen in his dean's dalmatic. The whole effect is remarkably beautiful; the semi-circles at the top of the picture and elsewhere make the rectangles seem larger. (Fol. 60v).

Onuerte nos deus salutaris noster. Et auerte iram tuam a nobis. Deus in adiuto rium meum

THE FALL OF THE REBEL ANGELS

The reader is doubtless aware that the demons are actually angels who, following the most beautiful amongst their number, Lucifer, rebelled against God. The vocation of all the angels is to celebrate the glory of the Almighty. The artist has naturally symbolized this activity by showing them seated in rows in the choirstalls, like monks or canons chanting the holy office in a chapel or cathedral. The numerous empty seats are those of the rebels, who were promptly hurled head first downwards; as they fell they caught fire and thus brought into being the flames of hell. The squad of warriors, under the throne of God, are the "celestial militia"; their role does not seem to be essential. This miniature is the third plate in the manuscript; it was inserted at the head of the Penitential Psalms. (Fol. 64v).

THE PROCESSION OF SAINT GREGORY

Here the illuminator gives new proof of his independence: whereas the margins were usually left blank or decorated with scrolls, or, sometimes, with fantastic themes, he has chosen to fill them, on this double page as well as a column without text, with a large figurative composition. The subject lent itself to the special shape thus imposed on the picture: a procession of small figures, which fit easily into a lower horizontal strip, passing in front of a number of tall monuments at least part of which fit into the vertical blanks. This is the procession which Pope St Gregory the Great ordered to proceed around the walls of Rome in 590 in order to obtain from Heaven the end of the plague which had been

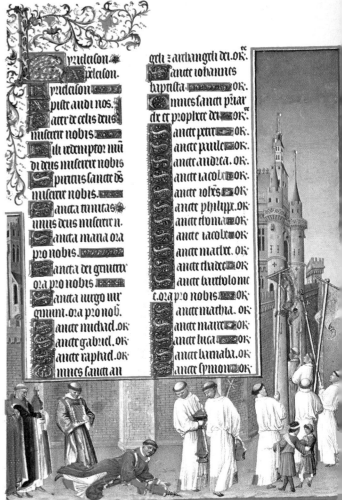

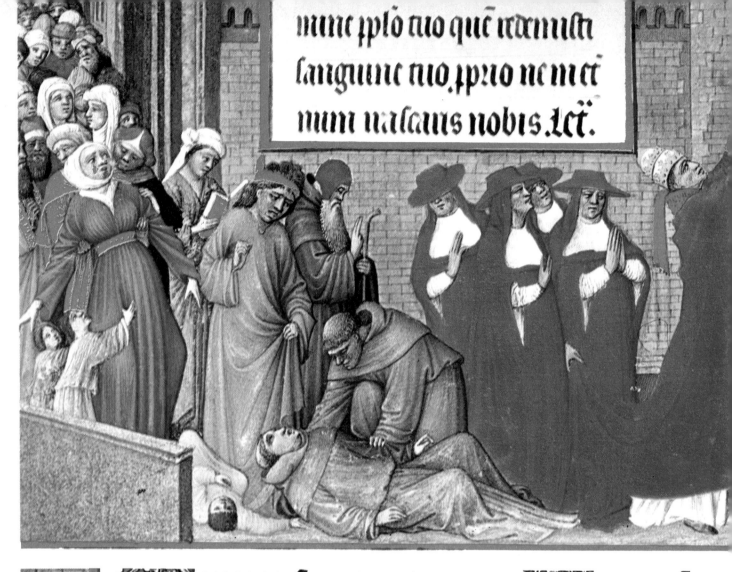

mine xpo tuo que redemisti
sanguine tuo, xpo ne met
num nascaris nobis. tet.

omnes sancti an   Sancte spn

laying waste the city. The reader will recognize the pontiff, who is walking behind a shrine containing relics, praying as he goes, and followed by four cardinals. He seems to notice, on top of Hadrian's mausoleum, an angel who is returning his bloodstained sword to its scabbard. This is a sign that the divine anger is placated. Henceforth the monument was to be known as Sant'Angelo. But the plague went on killing: its victims include a dean, wearing a blue dalmatic, who was carrying a small reliquary, and, behind the cardinals, a monk and a young boy. A woman dressed in blue seems distinctly unwell, to the evident distress of her two children. The monuments of Rome are depicted without much concern for accuracy. (Fol. 71v-72).

THE FUNERAL OF RAYMOND DIOCRES

Raymond Diocres, canon of Notre-Dame in Paris, an eloquent preacher, of very pious habits, was held to be a saintly man. He died. During the mass for the eternal repose of his soul, he lifted the lid of his coffin and said: "I have been condemned to the just judgment of God". The congregation was speechless with astonishment. The strip at the bottom of the illustrates the *Lay of the three dead men and the three live men*. The borders contain medallions depicting the death and scenes from the life of St Bruno, founder of the order of the Carthusians, who, according to legend, was prompted to withdraw to the solitary life by the terrifying story of Raymond Diocres. This miniature illustrates the Office of the Dead. (Fol. 86v).

VICTORY OF DAVID

David's warriors are clad in breastplates of gold, while the armor of their dastardly enemies are a tarnished steely grey. It is difficult to understand why they have left the backs of their thighs exposed. In any case the winners take advantage of this fact... The enemy horseman, on the right, seems to have had his right forearm cut off. The best part of this painting is undoubtedly the landscape, which provides a restful contrast to the bloody *mêlée* taking place in the foreground. (Fol. 95).

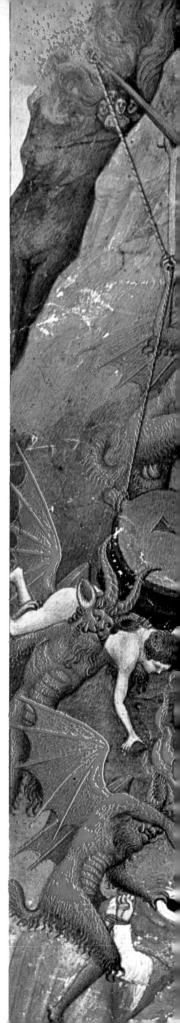

HELL

According to one 19th-century commentator, this painting seems to be directly inspired by the frescoes of Orcagna in the Campo Santo, Pisa. In actual fact, however, any medieval artist wishing to paint Hell had countless sources and models to choose from. Perhaps the flaming breath of Leviathan, who drags a dozen of the damned with him as he rises, may be the most original detail. One thing that is most definitely *not* original is the disproportionately large number of tonsured clerics, of all levels, who deserved the eternal flames: medieval man had no illusions about the saintliness of most of their clergy. Curiously enough, the faces do not express atrocious suffering. Instead, they are sad and almost resigned. This fact, however, does nothing to lessen the horrific effect of the whole scene, which is further enhanced by inspired use of lighting. This miniature is a plate added to the Office of the Dead. (Fol. 108).

the heavens opened and the Spirit descending upon him like a dove; and a voice came from heaven, "Thou art my beloved Son; with thee I am well pleased". Jean Colombe has condensed in his painting the two phases of the account given in the Gospel according to St Mark: John is still baptizing Jesus when the dove is already coming down from the heavens. He has depicted in the "open" sky the Father, whereas the Evangelist mentions only his voice. He has given him the appearance of a man in the prime of life, and not an old man, as he is painted by the artist of the Paradise on Earth (see page 46). The angels, on the left, , carrying Christ's clothes, are traditional but inappropriate. In this as in other paintings by Jean Colombe, the landscape with its bluish-tinted background is the aspect of his work which is to be preferred, even though the technique used may be considered somewhat too systematic. (Fol. 109v).

THE BAPTISM OF CHRIST

"In those days Jesus came from Nazareth of Galilee and was baptized by John in the Jordan. And when he came up out of the water, immediately he saw

PURGATORY

Jean Colombe has chosen not to emphasize the theme of horror when painting the place where the dead who have been assured of eternal bliss go to be purified. It is true that they suffer, but hope never leaves them and is revived each time they see one of their companions in misfortune, finally cleansed of all imperfections, lifted from the river of fire or the pool of ice by an angel who then takes him up to Paradise. The pure blue of the sky, the soft light with which the whole scene is imbued, the attractive female bodies unmarked by the cruel punishments presumably inflicted on those in Purgatory, all help lessen the painful effect of the torment of purification. (Fol. 113v).

THE BLESSED SACRAMENT

In this magnificent interior of a Gothic church a priest, with his acolyte, is celebrating the rite of the Blessed Sacrament, in the choir which is separated from the nave of the church by a rood-screen. He is wearing a cope, as was customary on such occasions. He seems to be hiding the monstrance, in which he is to raise the consecrated host for the adoration of the faithful, until the last possible moment. In the fore-ground, looking towards the choir, three men of oriental appearance are standing on the right; they are probably figures from the Old Testament who were regarded as having in a sense anticipated the Eucharist. One of them carries a loaf of bread and the other a vase which might contain wine. Some authors have seen in them Melchisedech, Moses and Elias. To the left, the bare-headed men are the three evangelists who described the Last Supper, the meal at which Christ instituted the Eucharist: Matthew, Mark and Luke. At the bottom, before a splendid row of 15th-century houses, St Anthony of Padua refutes a man's denial of the Real Presence by presenting the host to a mule, which promptly kneels down and will not touch the oats which the saint offers to him with the other hand. (Fol. 129v).

THE FINDING OF THE CROSS

The reader will doubtless remember that the cross to which Jesus was nailed was found by Helen, mother of the emperor Constantine. According to the legend three crosses were found in the ground at Calvary. The one on which Christ was executed was recognized by means of the healing power it possessed and which saved a women who was thought to be close to death. The lady in the long cloak who falls to her knees and raises her hands is apparently Helen. Here again we have a fine landscape. (Fol. 133v).

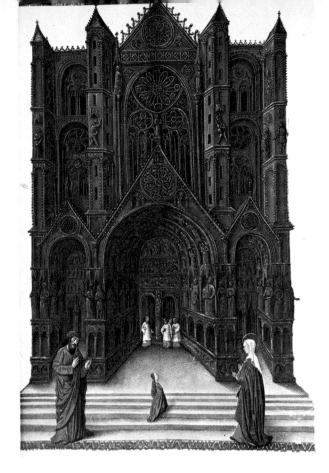

THE PRESENTATION OF THE VIRGIN

St Joachim and St Ann, the father and mother of Mary, have taken the young girl to the foot of the steps leading to the Temple, which she then ascends alone without the slightest hesitation. The priests await her under the portico. They are wearing surplices like Catholic priests and the Temple of Jerusalem is shown as the central part of the façade of the Cathedral of Bourges, freely rendered. As he has done in most of his large miniatures, Jean Colombe, rather than keeping a space at the bottom of the page for several lines of text, has preferred to make the beginning of this prayer an integral part of his composition: here it is seen on a strip which may be the first of the steps of the Temple. (Fol. 137).

MAP OF ROME

It is impossible to say why this plate has been inserted in the manuscript, between the minor offices of the week and the Hours of the Passion. This picture of the most famous medieval city of the Western world is contained in a fresco painted by Taddeo di Bartolo in the vestibule of the interior chapel of the communal palace of Sienna. This rather fanciful and stylized view of Rome is arranged with the north at the bottom of the picture: at the top, slightly to the right, is St Paul-outside-the-walls, which is situated to the south-west. Saint Mary Major, the bluish-white building with two pink roofs, two towers with tall spires and a crenellated rampart, is about half-way up the circle, slightly to the left, between the two branches of the aqueduct. At the end of one of those branches is the blank outline of the equestrian statue of Marcus Aurelius, which was later moved to the Capitol. Before the horse's nose stands the Colisseum, which has been transformed into a multistory tower. Slightly to the right, the Palatine has equipped, incongruously, with Gothic flying buttresses. Lower down, on another green mound, is the Capitol, in a fairly lifelike representation, next to a gibbet with a dead body hanging from it. Between the two mounds is St Francis Roman. To the left, the blank rectangle is still waiting to be filled in with the group of Dioscures. To the right of the Tiber—complete with the Tiberine Island and its two bridges— lies the Transteverene district and, below, the Vatican. At the bottom, on the banks of the Tiber, is the Milvius Bridge, near which, in 312, Constantine, the first Christian emperor, defeated his rival Maxentius; further to the right, the Castle of Sant'Angelo which is shown rather a long way from its bridge. The ground within the city walls is bare between the monuments, as if there were no houses at all in Rome It is depicted here as a cobblestone pavement such as those of the towns of Flanders with which the Limbourg brothers were familiar. (Fol. 141v).

THE ARREST OF JESUS

This is the first of the miniatures which illustrate the Hours of the Passion. The artist's rendering of the arrest of Jesus is based on the version contained in the Gospel of St John: "So Judas, procuring a band of soldiers and some officers from the chief priests and the Pharisees, went there with lanterns and torches and weapons. Then Jesus... said to them: Whom do you seek? They answered him: Jesus of Nazareth. Jesus answered: I told you that I am he... They drew back and fell to the ground".

The three other Gospels do not mention this collective fall. The blue night sky, dotted with stars and crossed by one or two shooting stars is unique in medieval illuminated manuscripts, providing, as it does, a backdrop for a dramatic scene which, though painted in dark and rather undifferentiated tones and barely illuminated by the glow of the torches, is nonetheless readily decipherable. (Fol. 142).

THE ARRIVAL AT THE PRETORIUM

The high priests and the Sanhedrin, assembled in the middle of the night to judge Christ, have concluded that he deserves death. But the final decision must be taken by Pilate, the procurator of Judea, representing Rome, the occupying power. As the dim light of dawn begins to fill the night sky, the servants of the priests and the Roman soldiers lead Christ to the pretorium. The artist has here painted, with evident relish, an urban landscape strongly reminiscent of his native Limbourg rather than a town in Asia Minor. The oriental flavor is provided by all the turbans and the pointed hats; on the other hand, the helmets and chainmail worn by the legionaries are distinctly Western. (Fol. 143).

THE SCOURGING OF CHRIST

Pilate cannot see what harm has been done by the man brought to him by the priests, and hopes to calm the fury of the Jews by having him scourged, without having to kill him. In his presence Christ is tied to a column of the pretorium and flogged with canes. The artist has also added a whip with several thongs, each having a spiked ball at the end, which is being used by the man in blue on the right. Pilate, with his abundant beard and his tall hairstyle, is as unlike a Roman governor as he could possibly be: in the Middle Ages Romans were depicted as subjects of the emperor of the East, the *basileus* of Byzantium, who was in fact the sole direct successor of the Caesars. Note the Jewish priests who are trying to enlist Pilate's assistance in their plans. On the far right, St John is taking notes for use in his Gospel. At the top of the columns, the statuettes of a naked man and woman are perhaps intended to represent the deities of the pagan Roman Pilate. (Fol. 144).

CHRIST IS TAKEN AWAY

Having been sent off to his death by Pilate who yielded to the Jews, Christ is led out of the pretorium, followed by another prisoner, probably one of the two thieves between whom he was to be crucified. The artist's imagination has made him paint here a building quite unlike the one into which Christ had originally been taken. His treatment of this scene is even more lavish in both architecture and dress. In fact the only person clad in simple garb is Christ. Note that he is not wearing the crown of thorns which was a characteristic feature of the Way of the Cross for several centuries thereafter. The faces of those taking Christ away and of the spectators are not filled with hatred; instead, they are serious. The four children on the left who are crowded around a tall oriflamme-bearer seem by far the least concerned of all. (Fol. 146v).

99

THE CRUCIFIXION

This film of the Passion in the manner of the Limbourg brothers is here unexpectedly interrupted by the style of Jean Colombe. The work thus loses in grace, charm and aesthetic qualities, especially as the artist is less inspired in this painting than in most of the others he contributed to this manuscript. A closer look, however, is rewarding: there is a special quality about the faces which are looking up towards the divine victim; there is a subtle difference of expression between the good thief on the left—to the right of Christ—and the bad thief; one is particularly impressed by the physiognomy of St John, which is certainly better rendered than that of the tearful Virgin whose back he is supporting. The skull and bones are apparently those of Adam; they happened to be at the precise spot chosen for the erection of the cross. (Fol. 152v).

THE DARKNESS

"It was now about the sixth hour, and there was darkness over the whole land until the ninth hour." Thus reads the Gospel according to Luke; Matthew and Mark say more or less the same thing. The artist, this time a Limbourg, has proved able to give this unaccustomed darkness a very different appearance than on the night of the Arrest. The darkness seems impenetrable. The dazzling halo of the crucified Christ loses none of its glow, the sun and the moon struggle to shine through and the darkness remains completely alien to the blazing glory of the Father, into whose hands the Son of God is about to surrender his soul. The three small medallions contain what appears to be an astronomer observing the phenomenon, the curtain of the temple rent asunder (Matthew, Mark, Luke), and the dead rising from their graves (Matthew). (Fol. 153).

CHRIST IS TAKEN DOWN FROM THE CROSS

Joseph of Arimathea, dressed in green, on the left ladder, receives the body of Christ in the "clean" shroud (Matthew) which he has brought with him; the man in pink wearing a turban is perhaps Nicodemus, who according to John, brought a mixture of myrrh and aloes to anoint the body. The man in blue seems to be hammering at the nail which went through the feet to remove it from the wood of the cross. The thieve's calves are covered with blood because Pilate, at the request of the Jews, had their legs broken (John). At the foot of the cross, Mary Magdalen. To the right, the other holy women. One of them holds in her hand the two nails which have already been removed and also a piece of precious linen. The Virgin looks on solemnly; she is no longer weeping. Behind her St John stretches out his arms to receive the body. The three children show the same lack of emotion as in a previous scene, that of Christ leaving the pretorium. Theirs is a pitiless age. (Fol. 156v).

CHRIST IS LAID IN THE SEPULCHRE

Once again the style of Jean Colombe. In the manuscript this scene is situated opposite the Descent from the Cross, by the Limbourg brothers. And it compares very well. In this most tragic of twilight hours the postures and expressions of the characters fully express their sentiments. One is particularly moved by the profile of Mary Magdalen, who is busy anointing the hand of her beloved Master with the ointment brought by Nicodemus. The body of Christ has already become rigid. It reminds one most distinctly of the *Pieta* of Avignon. (Fol. 157).

THE MASS

The last part of the *Très Riches Heures* presents the "proper" of a certain number of masses, that is the prayers peculiar to each of these masses; the "ordinary" remained unchanged. The first miniature in the series, which appears at the head of the proper of the third mass for Christmas, naturally depicts the mass itself. Following on a number of grandiloquent scriptural quotations, it is valuable particularly for its documentary qualities. We can see that the mass was celebrated exactly as it used to be until recently, when the altar was turned around to face the people. The celebrant is assisted by two acolytes dressed in the dalmatic of deacons. On the left, the canons are kneeling in their stalls. On the right, the choir sings at the lectern. One wonders as to the identity of the little man dressed in blue with red hose, the reason why his head is covered, and the exact nature of the weapon he is holding in his hand. Could he be what later came to be known as "the Swiss Guard"? The two ladies in the foreground seem to be seated on stools; the rest of the congregation is either standing or kneeling on the ground. The sculpted angel on the vault key bears the arms of the duke of Savoy, for whom Jean Colombe used to work. The three others, one of whom holds a paten, are of course imaginary. (Fol. 158).

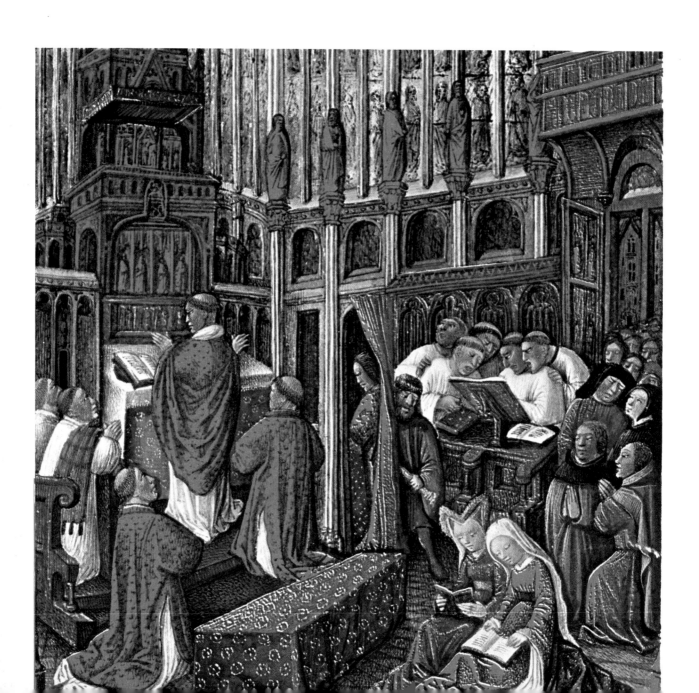

T er natus   super humanum cius et no
est nobis et   cabitur nomen cius ma
filius datus   gni consilij angelus. ps
est nobis cuius imperium   antate domino canti

THE TEMPTATION OF CHRIST

This is the illustration of the Gospel for the first Sunday in Lent. It is, at the same time, an admission—perhaps unintentional—that John of France, duke of Berry, with his seventeen princely residences, his jewels, his collections of gold and silver, his fine manuscripts and all the rest is situated precisely in this world where Satan rules. The author of this miniature, the style of which makes it the most archaic of the entire manuscript—had to depict Christ transported to the top of a high mountain by the Devil, who said to him, while showing him all the kingdoms of the world in all their glory: "All these things I shall give to you, if you fall down at my feet and worship me." And what did the artist choose, to symbolize this domain over which the Devil had such control? None other than the most beautiful of the duke's châteaux, that of Mehun-sur-Yèvre, where he kept, amongst other riches, the finest part of his library. With a little good will one can recognize in

the other buildings in this landscape other dwellings of the same duke. All that remains today of the splendid château of Mehun is a few dipalidated towers. (Fol. 161v).

THE CANAANITE WOMAN

This Canaanite woman, to use the description given by Matthew, was actually a Syrophoenician, according to Mark; at any rate she did not belong to the Chosen People. Even so she came to implore Christ to drive out a demon with which her daughter was possessed. But he replied: "I have been sent only for the sheep of the house of Israel." She insisted, however, and he said: "It is not right to take the children's bread and throw it to the dogs." She was not discouraged and came up with the words which the occasion called for: "Yes, Lord; yet even the dogs under the table eat the children's crumbs." This time Jesus yielded: "Or this saying you may go your way; the demon has left your daughter." In two registers of unequal width Jean Colombe has summarized this story. He has surpassed himself in the rendering of the landscape, offering us one of the most concrete views which we now have of the medieval, or more specifically the Savoy landscape. (Fol. 164).

...uli mei semper

...ad dominum et

...pr euellet de laqo

THE EXPLUSION OF THE DEMON

This miniature illustrates a brief passage from the Gospel of St Luke: "He was expelling a dumb demon. Once the demon had left the man's body he began to speak, and the crowds were filled with admiration." The rest of the text is a discussion with those who argued that Christ was in connivance with the demon Beelzebub. This is the Gospel for the fourth Sunday of Lent. Note the miniature devil coming out of the head of the possessed man, solidly belted. Although the text does not actually say so, the spectators, all of them dressed lavishly in the oriental style, were obviously, in the artist's mind, scribes and Pharisees. Behind the elegant and complex building which serves as a setting for this scene, the reader will note that the background, which could simply be the sky, is dark blue with branches. (Fol. 166).

THE MIRACLE OF THE LOAVES AND FISHES

The same artist who was unable to leave the Virgin in the poverty of the crib, or at least his very similar brother, has given an unashamedly luxurious treatment to the famous theme of the miracle of the loaves and fishes. The crowd, which the Evangelists estimated to be about five thousand strong could hardly have been wearing the sumptuous garments which occur so often at least in the right part of the painting. The Gospel says nothing, moreover, about the presence of the high priest: yet there he is, in the front row, distinguished by the characteristic emblem he wears on his chest. The people on the left, among whom are the man with the five loaves and the child with the two fishes, are more modestly dressed. The lush grass which covers all the ground visible in the picture is doubtless based on the actual words of the Gospel according to St Mark in which Christ ordered the people to sit down on the green grass in groups. Here again the sky is replaced by a blue background with branches; note also the delightful decorative work in the margin. (Fol. 168v).

Et aterilicula   gaudeteain leticia qui i
lem et conuie   tristicia fuistis ut exultetis
tnum faciett   et faciamini ab uberibus
omnes quidiligitis eam   consolacionis uir. ℔.

THE ENTRY INTO JERUSALEM

Palm Sunday, which comes just before Easter, commemorates Christ's triumphant entry into Jerusalem, shortly before his Passion. The four Evangelists give roughly similar accounts of this event. The miniature is based more precisely on the version according to St Matthew: the three other Gospels talk only of one donkey, whereas here we see Christ riding on a female donkey accompanied by her calf. The apostles, headed by St Peter and most of them recognizable only by their halo, follow close behind. The small figure perched in the tree would, at first sight, appear to be Zacheas, collector of Roman taxes at Jericho, who, on account of his short stature, had climbed onto a sycamore to get a better view of Christ's entry. But it is not him; it is undoubtedly a young boy; he can clearly be seen cutting branches from the tree to strew them in Christ's path. The facial expressions of the inhabitants —joy, trust, hope—are astonishingly accurate. Once again, the artist has given free rein to his architectural imagination, which, on this occasion, is somewhat Italianate in inspiration. (Fol. 173v).

THE RESURRECTION

When dealing with the Resurrection the artists had to rely entirely on their own imaginations, as the Gospels tell us only what happened after it. Curiously enough, Jean Colombe has given his Christ rising from the grave the pose that he himself, in the double scroll of the lower margin, and many other artists—such as the illuminator of the *Vita Christi* of Ludolph the Carthusian, roughly of the same period—have given to Christ after his resurrection when he appeared to Mary Magdalen in a garden, saying: "Do not touch me" *(noli me tangere)*. The gesture of the right arm suggests the presence of someone to whom he was speaking, so the artist has placed on top of the tomb an angel who seems uncertain as to which expression he should adopt. He clearly felt more at ease painting the guards posted by Pilate at the tomb on the request of the Jews: at the sight of the angel the guards "trembled and became like dead men" (Matthew). He has done a particularly masterly job rendering the sky just before dawn, with clouds beginning to turn pink as sunrise approaches. (Fol. 182v).

Eluntri et ad   tuam allcluia mirabilis
huic teaum   facta est fatentia tua alla
sum allelu   alleluia. psalmus
va posuisti super me manu   Domine probasti me z

SAINT MICHAEL

The last great miniature of the *Très Riches Heures* is once again in the style of the Limbourg brothers. The struggle in the heavens, so briefly described in the Apocalypse (Chapter XII), between St Michael and the "dragon" is situated by the artist above the most famous sanctuary in honor of the saint: the abbey of Mont-Saint-Michel, where the duke went as a pilgrim, with his nephew King Charles VI, on at least two occasions. This painting is an archeological document of rare accuracy. The Mount is shown at low tide: the boats with the curved prow and even a sailboat are aground on the sand. The pointed rock on the right is the Ile de Tombelaine, and "Mont Tombe", an important site in pre-Christian religion—as was Mont-Saint-Michel itself. In the margins the angels in the medallions may be intended to take the places of those who, in the Apocalypse, are fighting under the orders of St Michael. (Fol. 195).

Designed and produced by
Productions Liber SA

© Productions Liber SA
CH - Fribourg, 1979
and Editions Minerva SA
CH - Genève, 1979

Printed by
Officine Grafiche
de Aldo Garzanti Editore s.p.a.
Printed in Italy

First English edition published by Productions Liber S.A.
and Editions Minerva S.A., Fribourg - Genève.

Library of Congress Catalog
Card Number N.D. 3363. B. 5 T. 72 745, 6 '7 0944 79-10957

I.S.B.N. 0-517-282887

This edition is published by Crescent Books,
a division of Crown Publishers, Inc.

a   b   c   d   e   f   g   h